Let's eat Lunch

Clare Hibbert

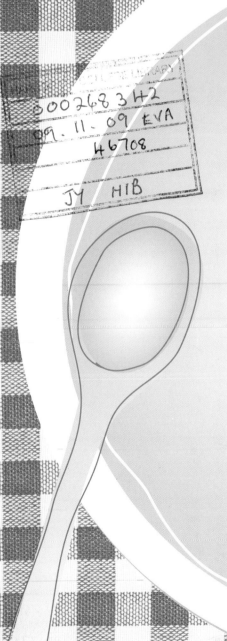

Published by Evans Brothers Limited
2A Portman Mansions
Chiltern Street
London W1U 6NR

Reprinted 2009
© Evans Brothers Limited 2007

Produced for Evans Brothers Limited by
White-Thomson Publishing Ltd

Printed in Hong Kong by New Era Printing Co. Ltd

Educational consultant: Sue Palmer MEd FRSA FEA
Project manager: Clare Hibbert
Picture research: Amy Sparks
Design: Balley Design Limited
Creative director: Simon Balley
Designer/Illustrator: Michelle Tilly

British Library Cataloguing in Publication Data

Hibbert, Clare 1970–
        Let's eat lunch. - (Sparklers) 1. Luncheons - Pictorial works - Juvenile
        literature 2. Food habits - Pictorial works - Juvenile literature
        I. Title
        394.1'5

ISBN: 978 0 2375 3380 9

Contents

Lunch time

crrr–unch!

This book is about lunch.

What time do **you** eat your lunch?

5

Eating together

Do you **eat** your lunch at school?

Who do **you** sit with?

chatter!

chatter!

Sandwiches

munch

What's your favourite sandwich?

When do you eat lunch
with your family?

Hot and Cold

blow

Soup warms you up

on a cold day.

Lunch outside

sizzle

Barbecues are for cooking food outside.

14

Lunch in China

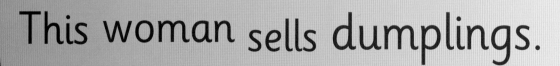

This woman sells dumplings.

Something sweet

Tasty!

Do you eat fruit after lunch?

apple tree

Can you think of any fruits

that grow on trees?

Lunchtime drinks

splash!

What do you drink with lunch?

slurp

smoothie

Milkshakes and smoothies taste good!

19

Make it: Greek Salad

Mix these things together to make a Greek salad.

- feta cheese ✓
- cucumber ✓
- tomato ✓
- olives ✓
- yellow pepper ✓
- olive oil ✓
- lemon juice ✓

Eat it with tasty pitta bread.

Notes for adults

Sparklers books are designed to support and extend the learning of young children. The books' high-interest subjects link in to the Early Years curriculum and beyond. Find out more about Early Years and reading with children from the National Literacy Trust (www.literacytrust.org.uk).

Themed titles
Let's eat Lunch is one of four **Food We Eat** titles that explore food and meals from around the world. The other titles are:
Let's eat Breakfast   Let's eat Dinner   Celebration Food

Areas of learning
Each **Food We Eat** title helps to support the following Foundation Stage areas of learning:
Personal, Social and Emotional Development
Communication, Language and Literacy
Mathematical Development
Knowledge and Understanding of the World
Creative Development

Reading together
When sharing this book with younger children, take time to explore the pictures together. Encourage children by asking them to find, identify, count or describe different objects. Point out different colours or textures.

Allow quiet spaces in your reading so that children can ask questions or repeat your words. Try pausing mid-sentence so children can predict the next word. This sort of participation develops early reading skills.

Follow the words with your finger as you read them aloud. The main text is in Infant Sassoon, a clear, friendly font specially designed for children learning to read and write. The labels and sound effects on the pages add fun, engage the reader and give children the opportunity to distinguish between different levels of communication. Where appropriate, labels, sound effects or main text may be presented in phonic spelling. Encourage children to imitate the sounds.

As you read the book, you can also take the opportunity to talk about the book itself with appropriate vocabulary, such as "page", "cover", "back", "front", "photograph", "label" and "page number".

You can also extend children's learning by using the books as a springboard for discussion and further activities. There are a few suggestions on the facing page.

Pages 4–5: Lunch time
Encourage children to keep a food diary, either as a group or individually. Divide a big piece of paper into seven sections, one for each day of the week. Each afternoon, encourage children to draw, paint or stick photos of what they ate for lunch.

Pages 6–7: Eating together
Ask children to draw a picture of their lunch table, and help them to write the names of who sits where. They can add images of what they like eating best for lunch and appropriate cutlery in the right places. Discuss table manners and allow children to practise asking for things.

Pages 8–9: Sandwiches
Make pretend sandwiches using thin coloured foam or painted card for the bread and ingredients. You could role-play a sandwich "bar". Ask children to sort the ingredients into different containers. Two children can play servers, assembling sandwiches to order. The others can be customers, queuing, choosing, ordering and paying for their lunches.

Pages 10–11: Lunch at home
The photograph on the page shows a Japanese family using chopsticks. Provide the children with chopsticks and small pieces of food, such as raisins, to pick up and eat.

Pages 12–13: Hot and cold
Grow a salad ingredient together. Cress is simplest and can be grown in yoghurt pots on a sunny windowsill at any time of the year. However, if you have the space available and it's the right season, why not grow tomatoes in bags or pots? Cherry tomatoes are especially appealing to young children.

Pages 14–15: Lunch outside
Teach the children the words and music to the "Teddy bears' picnic" – if they don't know it already. Then organise a pretend teddy bears' picnic using tea-set plates and cups, and pretend foods (plastic, wood, or homemade from saltdough).

Pages 16–17: Something sweet
Make some fruity jigsaws. Find big photos of fruit, stick on to card for strength and then cut up to make jigsaw pieces.

Pages 18–19: Lunchtime drinks
Provide a plastic jug of water and containers so children can practise pouring. Turn this into a musical activity for older children by using glass beakers, filled with different amounts of water. Children can tap the side of each glass gently with a wooden spoon to produce notes of different pitches.

Pages 20–21: Make it: Greek salad
Organise a blind tasting of different salad ingredients, such as tomatoes, cucumber, lettuce, radish, celery, sweet peppers, avocado and grated carrot. See which ones children can identify.

23

Index

Picture acknowledgements:
Alamy: 6-7 (Rob Wilkinson), 12 (Real World People), 15 (Tina Manley), 20-21 (© Profimedia International s.r.o.); **Corbis:** cover tablecloth, 2-3, 22-24 (Gregor Schuster), 10-11 (Redlink), 18 (Sean Justice); **Evans:** 9 (Gareth Boden); **Getty:** cover (StockFood Creative), 4-5 (Vanessa Davies), 13 (Peter Dazeley/The Image Bank), 16 (Anne Ackermann); **iStockphoto:** cover sky (Judy Foldetta), 17, 19 (Olga Lyubkina); **Photolibrary:** 8 (Pacific Stock), 14 (Foodpix).

With special thanks to Nicky and Luke Parker for the use of the photograph on page 9.